Vegan Soup Cookbook

Delicious Vegan Soup Recipes for Better Health and Easy Weight Loss

By Heather Ozpetek

Sommario

Introduction

Vegetarianism refers to a lifestyle that excludes the consumption of all forms of meat, including pork, chicken, beef, lamb, venison, fish and shells.

According to the preference and belief of different people different degrees of vegetarianism were born, in fact there are some people who like to use at least animal derivatives and others who instead take their beliefs to the extreme by eliminating even the derivatives and are called vegans.

Vegetarianism as well as being a beautiful mission of life and demonstration of respect for nature is also good for the respect of our bodies by reducing the risk of chronic diseases.

Have fun with our fantastic recipes

Soups

Borlotti Bean and Sun-dried Tomato Soup

Ingredients

1 pound borlotti beans, sorted and rinsed 1 1/2 quarts vegetable stock

½ quart water

1 medium onion, diced

9 cloves of garlic, peeled and smashed 2 tsp sea salt

1/4 tsp pepper

2 medium potatoes, diced

1 pound frozen, sliced carrots

1 cup chopped sun-dried tomatoes* 1-2 tsp lime juice

3-4 tbsp fresh, minced parsley

Add the beans, veggie stock and water, onion, garlic, salt and pepper in a pot and cook over low-medium heat.

Simmer for 3-4 hours.

When the beans become soft, add the potato and simmer

until the potatoes become tender.

Add the carrots, tomatoes and lime juice and cook until heated through.

Add the parsley.

Season with more salt and pepper.

Smoky Summer Squash and Carrot Soup

Ingredients

1 medium summer squash (1 lb of peeled and cubed butternut squash)

1 medium red onion, diced

1/2 lb carrots, peeled and cut into chunks 1 Fuji apple, peeled and sliced

3 cups vegetable stock 1 cup vegetable broth 1 tsp. ground cumin

1 tsp salt

1 tsp. ground coriander 1/4 tsp dried ground sage Salt and pepper to taste

INSTRUCTIONS

Combine the squash, red onion, carrots, apple, broth, stock and bay leaf in slow cooker.

Cook for about 6 hours on low or until veggies are soft. Take the bay leaf and discard.

Transfer the ingredients of the slow cooker to a blender Blend until smooth.

Pour back into the slow cooker and season with salt, pepper, coriander, & cumin

Taste and season with more salt and pepper to taste.

Winter Squash Carrot and Parsnip Soup

Ingredients

1 medium wintersquash squash (1 lb of peeled and cubed butternutsquash)

1 medium red onion, diced

1/2 lb carrots, peeled and cut into chunks 1 parsnip, peeled and sliced

2 cups vegetable stock 1 tsp salt

1 tsp pepper

2 (13.5 oz) cans almond milk Salt and pepper to taste

Combine the squash, red onion, parsnips, carrots, & stock in slowcooker.

Cook for about 6 hours on low or until veggies are soft. Transfer the ingredients of the slow cooker to a blender Blend until smooth.

Pour back into the slow cooker and season with salt, pepper & sage Add the almond milk. Stir.

Taste and season with more salt and pepper to taste.

Chinese Butternut Squash Soup

Ingredients

1 medium butternut squash (1 lb of peeled and cubed butternut squash)

1 medium red onion, diced

1/2 lb carrots, peeled and cut into chunks 3 cloves garlic, minced

3 cups vegetable stock

4 tsp. Chinese five spice powder 1 tsp salt

1 tsp pepper

1 tsp. grated ginger

1 (13.5 oz) can vegetable broth 3 tbsp. sesame seed oil

Salt and pepper to taste

INSTRUCTIONS

Combine the squash, red onion, carrots, garlic, stock , sesame seed oil and bay leaf in slow cooker.

Cook for about 6 hours on low or until veggies are soft. Take the bay leaf and discard.

Transfer the ingredients of the slow cooker to a blender Blend until smooth.

Pour back into the slow cooker and season with salt, pepper & sage Add the coconut milk. Stir.

Taste and season with more salt and pepper to taste.

Carrot Apple and Summer Squash Soup

Ingredients

1 medium summer squash 1 medium red onion, diced

1/2 lb carrots, peeled and cut into chunks 1 Fuji apple, peeled and sliced

3 cups vegetable stock 1 bay leaf

1 tsp salt

1 tsp pepper

1/4 tsp dried ground sage

1 (13.5 oz) can almond milk Salt and pepper to taste

Combine the squash, red onion, carrots, apple, stock and bay leaf in slow cooker.

Cook for about 6 hours on low or until veggies are soft. Take the bay leaf and discard.

Transfer the ingredients of the slow cooker to a blender Blend until smooth.

Pour back into the slow cooker and season with salt, pepper & sage Add the almond milk. Stir.

Taste and season with more salt and pepper to taste.

Winter Squash Carrot and Cayenne Pepper Soup

Ingredients

1 medium winter squash

1 medium red onion, diced

1/2 lb carrots, peeled and cut into chunks 3 garlic cloves, minced

3 cups vegetable stock 1 tsp salt

1 tsp cayenne pepper 1/4 cup peanut butter

1 (13.5 oz) can coconut milk Salt and pepper to taste

INSTRUCTIONS

Combine the squash, red onion, carrots, peanut butter, garlic, stock and bay leaf in slow cooker.

Cook for about 6 hours on low or until veggies are soft. Take the bay leaf and discard.

Transfer the ingredients of the slow cooker to a blender Blend until smooth.

Pour back into the slow cooker and season with salt, pepper & sage Add the coconut milk. Stir.

Taste and season with more salt and cayenne pepper to taste.

Hubbard Squash Mushroom and Red Onion Soup

Ingredients

1 lb. Hubbard squash

1 medium red onion, diced

1/2 lb carrots, peeled and cut into chunks 1 can (14 oz.) mushrooms, sliced

3 cups vegetable stock 1 bay leaf

1 tsp salt

1 tsp pepper

2 sprigs rosemary

Salt and pepper to taste

INSTRUCTIONS

Combine the squash, red onion, carrots, mushrooms, stock and rosemary in slow cooker.

Cook for about 6 hours on low or until veggies are soft. Take the bay leaf and discard.

Transfer the ingredients of the slow cooker to a blender Blend until smooth.

Pour back into the slow cooker and season with salt & pepper Taste and season with more salt and pepper to taste.

Winter Squash and Carrots Soup

Ingredients

1 medium winter squash (1 lb of peeled and cubed butternut squash) 1 medium red onion, diced

1/2 lb carrots, peeled and cut into chunks 1 Fuji apple, peeled and sliced

3 cups vegetable stock 1 fresh tarragon

1 tsp salt

1 tsp pepper

1/4 tsp herbs de Provence Salt and pepper to taste

INSTRUCTIONS

Combine the squash, red onion, carrots, apple, stock and fresh tarragon in slow cooker.

Cook for about 6 hours on low or until veggies are soft.

Take the tarragon and discard.

Transfer the ingredients of the slow cooker to a blender
Blend until smooth.

Pour back into the slow cooker and season with salt,
pepper & herbs de Provence

Taste and season with more salt and pepper to taste.

Summer Squash Carrot and Red Onion Soup

Ingredients

1 medium summer squash (1 lb of peeled and cubed butternut squash)

1 medium red onion, diced

1/2 lb carrots, peeled and cut into chunks 3 cups vegetable stock

1 tsp salt

1 tsp pepper 1/4 tsp cumin

½ (6.5 oz) can tomatoes Salt and pepper to taste

INSTRUCTIONS

Combine the squash, red onion, carrots, & stock in slow cooker. Cook for about 6 hours on low or until veggies are soft.

Transfer the ingredients of the slow cooker to a blender Blend until smooth.

Pour back into the slow cooker and season with salt, pepper & cumin Add the tomatoes. Stir.

Taste and season with more salt and pepper to taste.

Lima Bean Soup

Ingredients

1 teaspoon extra virgin olive oil 1/2 cup chopped red onions

4 cloves garlic, minced 2 cups vegetable broth 1 cup salsa

1 14-ounce can lima beans

1 green bell pepper, chopped 1/2 teaspoon sea salt

1 avocado, chopped

1/2 cup loosely-packed cilantro Optional:

1/2 cup crumbled corn tortilla chips Chop onions and garlic.

Chop red bell pepper. Cook and Serve:

Heat the olive oil on medium.

Add the red onions and garlic to the pan and stir until softened, 3 to 5 minutes.

Pour in broth, salsa, bell peppers, black beans, and salt. Boil over high heat.

Reduce heat to low and simmer until heated through for about 5 minutes.

Top with half of the avocado, cilantro, and tortilla chips.

Garbanzo Bean Thai Curry Soup

Ingredients

1 teaspoon olive oil

1/2 cup chopped red onions 4 cloves garlic, minced

2 cups vegetable broth 1 tsp. curry powder

1 14-ounce can garbanzo beans 1/2 teaspoon sea salt

1 cup coconut milk

1/2 cup loosely-packed coriander

Heat the olive oil on medium.

Add the red onions and garlic to the pan and stir until softened, 3 to 5 minutes.

Pour in broth, curry powder, bell peppers, black beans, coriander coconut milk and salt.

Boil over high heat.

Reduce heat to low and simmer until heated through for about 5 minutes.

Sesame and Soy Bean Soup

Ingredients

1 teaspoon sesame oil

1/2 cup chopped red onions 4 cloves garlic, minced

2 cups vegetable broth

1 14-ounce can soy beans 1/2 teaspoon sea salt

Heat the sesame oil on medium.

Add the red onions and garlic to the pan and stir until softened, 3 to 5 minutes.

Pour in broth, black beans, and salt. Boil over high heat.

Reduce heat to low and simmer until heated through for about 5 minutes.

Pinto Bean Jalapeno Soup

Ingredients:

1 teaspoon extra virgin olive oil 1/2 cup chopped yellow onions 4 cloves garlic, minced

2 cups vegetable broth 1 cup salsa

1 14-ounce can pinto beans

¼ cup jalapeno peppers, chopped 1/2 teaspoon sea salt

1 cup corn

1 tsp. chili powder

Heat the olive oil on medium.

Add the yellow onions and garlic to the pan and stir until softened, 3 to 5 minutes.

Pour in broth, salsa, jalapeno peppers, black beans, and salt. Boil over high heat.

Reduce heat to low and simmer until heated through for about 5 minutes.

Top with the corn & chili powder.

Jalapeno Tortilla Soup

Ingredients:

1 teaspoon extra virgin olive oil 1/2 cup chopped red onions

4 cloves garlic, minced 2 cups vegetable broth 1 cup vegetable stock

1 14-ounce can black beans

1 jalapeno pepper, chopped 1/2 teaspoon sea salt

1 tbsp. apple cider vinegar Optional:

1/2 cup crumbled corn tortilla chips Chop onions and garlic.

Chop red bell pepper. Cook and Serve:

Heat the olive oil on medium.

Add the red onions and garlic to the pan and stir until softened, 3 to 5 minutes.

Pour in broth, stock, salsa, jalapeno peppers, black beans,

apple cider vinegar and salt.

Boil over high heat.

Reduce heat to low and simmer until heated through for about 5 minutes.

Lentil Tortilla Soup

Ingredients:

1 teaspoon extra virgin olive oil 1/2 cup chopped red onions

4 cloves garlic, minced 2 cups vegetable broth 1 cup salsa

1 tsp. Louisiana style hot sauce 1 14-ounce can lentils

1 jalapeno , chopped 1/2 teaspoon sea salt 1 avocado, chopped

1 tsp. cumin

½ tsp, coriander Optional:

1/2 cup crumbled corn tortilla chips Chop onions and garlic.

Chop red bell pepper.

Heat the olive oil on medium.

Add the red onions and garlic to the pan and stir until softened, 3 to 5 minutes.

Pour in broth, salsa, hot sauce, jalapeno peppers, black beans, cumin, coriander and salt.

Boil over high heat.

Reduce heat to low and simmer until heated through for about 5 minutes.

Top with half of the avocado, cilantro, and tortilla chips.

Vegan Chorizo and White Bean Tortilla Soup

Ingredients:

1 teaspoon extra virgin olive oil 1/2 cup chopped red onions

4 cloves garlic, minced 2 cups vegetable broth

1 cup coarsely chopped vegan chorizo 1 14-ounce can white beans

1 green bell pepper, chopped 1/2 teaspoon sea salt

1 tsp. cumin

1 tsp. paprika

1/2 cup loosely-packed cilantro Optional:

1/2 cup crumbled corn tortilla chips Chop onions and garlic.

Chop red bell pepper.

Heat the olive oil on medium.

Add the red onions and garlic to the pan and stir until softened, 3 to 5 minutes.

Pour in broth, chorizo, bell peppers, cumin, black beans, paprika, and salt.

Boil over high heat.

Reduce heat to low and simmer until heated through for about 5 minutes.

Mexican Garbanzo Bean Soup

Ingredients:

1 teaspoon extra virgin olive oil 1/2 cup chopped red onions

4 cloves garlic, minced 2 cups vegetable broth 1 tsp. cumin

1 14-ounce can garbanzo beans 1 green bell pepper, chopped 1/2 teaspoon sea salt

1 tbsp. lime juice

1/2 cup loosely-packed cilantro

1 cup vegan chorizo, coarsely chopped

Heat the olive oil on medium.

Add the red onions and garlic to the pan and stir until softened, 3 to 5 minutes.

Pour in broth, salsa, cumin, vegan chorizo, bell peppers, black beans, lime juice, and salt.

Boil over high heat.

Reduce heat to low and simmer until heated through for about 5 minutes.

Parsnip and Turnip Soup

Ingredients

1 tablespoon extra-virgin olive oil 3 teaspoons crushed garlic

1 tablespoon chopped fresh cilantro 1 teaspoon chili paste

1 red onion, chopped

3 large parsnips, peeled and sliced 1 large turnip, peeled and chopped 5 cups vegetable stock

Heat oil in a pot over medium heat. Cook garlic, cilantro and chili paste. Cook onions until tender.

Add the parsnips and turnip.

Cook for 5 minutes and pour in vegetable stock.

Simmer for 40 minutes, or until parsnips and turnip become soft. Blend until smooth.

Watercress and Carrot Soup

Ingredients

1 tablespoon sesame oil

3 teaspoons crushed garlic

1 tablespoon chopped fresh cilantro 2 teaspoons chili garlic sauce

1 red onion, chopped

3 large carrots, peeled and sliced

1 bunch watercress, coarsely chopped 5 cups vegetable stock

Heat oil in a pot over medium heat.

Cook garlic, cilantro and chili garlic sauce. Cook onions until tender.

Add the carrots and watercress.

Cook for 5 minutes and pour in vegetable stock.

Simmer for 40 minutes, or until spinach and carrots become soft. Blend until smooth.

Jalapeno Turnip and Carrot Soup

Ingredients

1 tablespoon extra-virgin olive oil 3 teaspoons crushed garlic

1 tablespoon chopped fresh cilantro 1 teaspoon jalapeno, minced

1 tsp. cumin

1 red onion, chopped

3 large carrots, peeled and sliced 1 large turnip, peeled and chopped 5 cups vegetable stock

Heat oil in a pot over medium heat.

Cook garlic, cilantro, cumin and jalapenos. Cook onions until tender.

Add the carrots and turnip.

Cook for 5 minutes and pour in vegetable stock.

Simmer for 40 minutes, or until turnip and carrots become soft. Blend until smooth.

Thai Turnip and Sweet Potato Soup

Ingredients

1 tablespoon sesame seed oil 3 teaspoons crushed garlic

1 tablespoon chopped fresh cilantro 1 teaspoon Thai bird chilies, minced 2 tbsp. tamarind paste

1 tsp. Thai chili paste 1 red onion, chopped

3 large turnips, peeled and sliced

1 large sweet potato, peeled and chopped 5 cups vegetable broth

Heat oil in a pot over medium heat.

Cook garlic, cilantro, Thai chilies, tamarind paste, and Thai chili paste.

Cook onions until tender. Add the turnips and potato.

Cook for 5 minutes and pour in vegetable stock.

Simmer for 40 minutes, or until potatoes and turnips become soft. Blend until smooth.

Ancho Chili Carrot and Turnip Soup

Ingredients

1 tablespoon extra-virgin olive oil 3 teaspoons crushed garlic

1 tablespoon chopped fresh cilantro 1 teaspoon lemon juice

1 teaspoon annatto seeds

½ tsp. cayenne pepper

1 teaspoon ancho chilies, finely minced 1 red onion, chopped

3 large carrots, peeled and sliced 1 large turnip, peeled and chopped 5 cups vegetable stock

Heat oil in a pot over medium heat.

Cook garlic, cilantro, lemon juice, annatto seeds, ancho chilies and cayenne pepper.

Cook onions until tender. Add the carrots and turnip.

Cook for 5 minutes and pour in vegetable stock.

Simmer for 40 minutes, or until turnip and carrots become soft. Blend until smooth.

Summer Squash and Lemon Grass Soup

Ingredients

1 tablespoon extra-virgin olive oil 3 teaspoons crushed garlic

1 tablespoon chopped fresh cilantro 2 to 3 stalks lemon

grass

1 tsp. ginger, finely minced 1 red onion, chopped

3 large summer squash, peeled and sliced 1 large potato, peeled and chopped

5 cups vegetable stock

Heat oil in a pot over medium heat.

Cook garlic, cilantro, lemon grass,& ginger. Cook onions until tender.

Add the squash and potato.

Cook for 5 minutes and pour in vegetable stock.

Simmer for 40 minutes, or until potatoes and squash become soft. Blend until smooth.

Hungarian Winter Squash and Carrot Soup

Ingredients

1 tablespoon olive oil

5 teaspoons crushed garlic

1 teaspoon Hungarian paprika 1 red onion, chopped

3 large carrots, peeled and sliced

1 large winter squash, peeled and chopped 5 cups vegetable stock

Heat oil in a pot over medium heat.

Cook garlic, cilantro and Hungarian paprika. Cook onions until tender.

Add the carrots and squash.

Cook for 5 minutes and pour in vegetable stock.

Simmer for 40 minutes, or until winter squash and carrots become soft.

Blend until smooth.

Summer Squash and Winter Soup

Ingredients

1 tablespoon sesame seed oil 7 teaspoons crushed garlic

1 tablespoon chopped fresh cilantro

1 teaspoon Chinese five spice powder 1 teaspoon chili garlic paste

1 red onion, chopped

3 large pcs. of summer squash, peeled and sliced 1 large winter squash, peeled and chopped

5 cups vegetable broth

Heat oil in a pot over medium heat. Cook garlic, cilantro and chili paste. Cook onions until tender.

Add the squash.

Cook for 5 minutes and pour in vegetable stock. Simmer for 40 minutes, or until squash become soft. Blend until smooth.

Poblano Chili and Summer Squash Soup

Ingredients

Poblano Soup Ingredients:

4 tablespoons salted butter

1 small red onion, coarsely chopped 1 large leek, white part only, sliced

1 green bell pepper, coarsely chopped

1 (or two if you like things spicy) small dry-roasted poblano chili, sliced

6 cloves garlic, diced

1 large summer squash, cubed (you can use two if you like your soup thick)

4 cups vegetable broth 1 cup cashews

1-1 /4 almond milk Sea salt

Black pepper

Optional garnish:

Sliced jalapeno pepper

Soak cashews in almond milk for an hour. Melt butter in a pan.

Add the red onion, leek, chilies, bell pepper, garlic, and summer squash.

Cook on low heat and stir until the onion is translucent, 6 1/2 minutes.

Add the broth into the pan.

Simmer until the summer squash are fork tender for about 25 minutes.

Take it off the heat.

Process the mixture in a blender until smooth. Return the soup to the pan.

In the blender, blend cashews with almond milk until smooth Add to the soup mixture.

Heat the soup on medium heat for a few more minutes.Garnish with slices of jalapeno.

Creamy Parsnip and Peanut Soup

Ingredients

Poblano Soup Ingredients:

4 tablespoons salted butter

1 small red onion, coarsely chopped 1 large leek, white part only, sliced

1 green bell pepper, coarsely chopped 5 pcs. Thai chilies, sliced

5 Thai basil leaves

2 tbsp. tamarind paste 8 cloves garlic, diced

1 large parsnip, cubed (you can use two if you like your soup thick) 4 cups vegetable broth

1 cup peanuts

1-1 /4 coconut milk Sea salt

Black pepper

Optional garnish:

Sliced jalapeno pepper

Soak peanuts in almond milk for an hour. Melt non-dairy butter in a pan.

Add the red onion, leek, chilies, Thai basil, tamarind paste, bell pepper, garlic, and potato.

Cook on low heat and stir until the onion is translucent, 6 1/2 minutes.

Add the broth into the pan.

Simmer until the parsnip are fork tender for about 25 minutes. Take it off the heat.

Process the mixture in a blender until smooth. Return the soup to the pan.

In the blender, blend peanuts with coconut milk until

smooth Add to the soup mixture.

Heat the soup on medium heat for a few more minutes. Garnish with slices of jalapeno.

Creamy Potato Soup

Ingredients

Poblano Soup Ingredients:

4 tablespoons salted butter

1 small red onion, coarsely chopped 1 large leek, white part only, sliced

1 green bell pepper, coarsely chopped

1 (or two if you like things spicy) small dry-roasted poblano chili, sliced

6 cloves garlic, diced 1 tbsp. annatto seeds

1 large potato, cubed (you can use two if you like your soup thick) 4 cups vegetable broth

½ cup half and half 1-1/4 milk

Sea salt Black pepper

Optional garnish:

Sliced jalapeno pepper

Melt non-dairy butter in a pan.

Add the red onion, leek, chilies, bell pepper, garlic, and potato. Cook on low heat and stir until the onion is translucent, 6 1/2 minutes.

Add the broth and annatto seeds into the pan.

Simmer until the potatoes are fork tender for about 25 minutes. Take it off the heat.

Process the mixture in a blender until smooth. Return the soup to the pan.

In the blender, blend peanut butter with almond milk until smooth Add to the soup mixture.

Heat the soup on medium heat for a few more minutes. Garnish with slices of jalapeno.

Lentil and Butternut Squash Curry Soup

Ingredients

1 tablespoon sesame seed oil 1 small red onion, chopped

1 tablespoon minced fresh ginger root 3 cloves garlic, chopped

1 pinch fenugreek seeds 1 cup dry red lentils

1 cup butternut squash - peeled, seeded, and cubed 1/3 cup finely chopped fresh cilantro

2 cups water

1/2 (14 ounce) can almond milk 2 tablespoons tomato paste

1 teaspoon red curry powder 1/4 cayenne pepper

1 pinch ground nutmeg salt and pepper to taste

Heat the oil in a pot over medium heat

Sauté the onion, garlic, and fenugreek until onion becomes tender. Add the lentils, squash, and cilantro into the pot.

Add the water, almond milk, and tomato paste.

Season with curry powder, cayenne pepper, nutmeg, salt, and pepper.

Boil and reduce heat to low

Simmer until lentils and squash are tender. For about 30 min.

Borlotti Bean and Squash Soup

Ingredients

1 tablespoon extra virgin olive oil 1 small red onion, chopped

3 cloves garlic, chopped 1 tbsp. lime juice

1 cup dry borlotti beans

1 cup butternut squash - peeled, seeded, and cubed 1/3 cup finely chopped fresh cilantro

2 cups water

1/2 (14 ounce) can almond milk 2 tablespoons annatto seeds

1 teaspoon cumin 1/4 cayenne pepper

1 pinch ground nutmeg salt and pepper to taste

Heat the oil in a pot over medium heat

Sauté the onion, garlic, annatto seeds and cumin until onion becomes tender.

Add the beans, squash, and cilantro into the pot. Add the water, almond milk and lime juice

Season with, cayenne pepper, nutmeg, salt, and pepper. Boil and reduce heat to low

Simmer until beans and squash are tender. For about 30 min.

Thai Curried Butternut Squash Soup

Ingredients

1 tablespoon sesame seed oil 1 small red onion, chopped

1 tablespoon minced fresh ginger root 3 cloves garlic, chopped

1 cup peanuts

1 cup butternut squash - peeled, seeded, and cubed 1/3 cup finely chopped fresh cilantro

2 cups water

1/2 (14 ounce) can coconut milk 1 teaspoon red curry powder 1tsp. Thai bird chilies

1 pinch ground nutmeg salt and pepper to taste

Heat the oil in a pot over medium heat

Sauté the onion, ginger, and garlic until onion becomes

tender. Add the peanuts, squash, and cilantro into the pot.

Add the water & coconut milk.

Season with curry powder, Thai bird chilies, nutmeg, salt, and pepper.

Boil and reduce heat to low

Simmer until peanuts and squash are tender. For about 30 min.

Spicy Summer Squash and Lentil Soup

Ingredients

1 tablespoon extra virgin olive oil 1 small red onion, chopped

3 cloves garlic, chopped 1 pinch fenugreek seeds 1 cup dry red lentils

1 cup summer squash - peeled, seeded, and cubed 1 cup water

1 cup vegetable stock

2 tablespoons tomato paste 1 teaspoon Italian seasoning 1/4 tsp. cayenne pepper

salt and pepper to taste

Heat the oil in a pot over medium heat

Sauté the onion, garlic, and fenugreek until onion becomes tender. Add the lentils and squash into the pot.

Add the water, vegetable stock and tomato paste.

Season with Italian seasoning, cayenne pepper, salt, and pepper. Boil and reduce heat to low

Simmer until lentils and squash are tender. For about 30 min.

Simple Carrot and Tarragon Soup

Ingredients

2 tablespoons extra virgin olive oil 1 small red onion, minced

1 medium carrot, peeled and thinly sliced 1 celery rib, thinly sliced

1/2 teaspoon dried tarragon 2 cups vegetable stock

1/4 cup wine vinegar

Heat the oil over medium-high heat.

Sauté red onions until tender for about 5 minutes. Slowly add carrots, celery, and tarragon

Cook for another 5 minutes, or until carrots become tender. Add vegetable broth and vinegar

Boil and simmer.

Cook for 15 minutes longer.

Chinese Turnip Soup

Ingredients

2 tablespoons sesame seed oil 1 small red onion, minced

1 small turnip, peeled and thinly sliced 1 celery rib, thinly sliced

1/2 teaspoon Chinese five spice powder 2 cups vegetable broth

1/4 cup rice wine

Heat the oil over medium-high heat.

Sauté red onions until tender for about 5 minutes. Slowly add turnip, celery, and five spice powder

Cook for another 5 minutes, or until turnip becomes tender. Add vegetable broth and rice wine

Boil and simmer.

Cook for 15 minutes longer.

Thai Carrot Soup

Ingredients

2 tablespoons sesame seed oil 1 small red onion, minced

1 small carrot, peeled and thinly sliced 1/2 teaspoon Thai chili paste

2 cups vegetable broth

1/4 cup coconut or white vinegar 1 sprig cilantro

Heat the oil over medium-high heat.

Sauté red onions until tender for about 5 minutes. Slowly add carrots and chili paste

Cook for another 5 minutes, or until carrots become tender. Add vegetable stock and vinegar

Boil and simmer.

Cook for 15 minutes longer. Garnish with cilantro

Spicy and Tangy Parsnip Soup

Ingredients

2 tablespoons extra virgin olive oil 1 small red onion, minced

1 small parsnip, peeled and thinly sliced 1 celery rib, thinly sliced

1/2 teaspoon cumin

½ teaspoon cayenne pepper 1 tsp. annatto seeds

1 tbsp. lime juice

2 cups vegetable stock

Heat the oil over medium-high heat.

Sauté red onions until tender for about 5 minutes.

Slowly add parsnip, celery, cumin, cayenne pepper, annatto seeds and lime juice

Cook for another 5 minutes, or until parsnip becomes tender. Add vegetable broth and vinegar

Boil and simmer.

Cook for 15 minutes longer.

Hungarian Carrot Soup

Ingredients

2 tablespoons extra virgin olive oil 1 small red onion, minced

1 medium carrot, peeled and thinly sliced 1 celery rib, thinly sliced

5 garlic cloves finely minced

1 teaspoon Hungarian paprika 2 cups vegetable stock

1/4 cup wine vinegar

Heat the oil over medium-high heat.

Sauté red onions until tender for about 5 minutes.

Slowly add carrots, celery, garlic cloves and Hungarian paprika Cook for another 5 minutes, or until carrots become tender.

Add vegetable broth and vinegar Boil and simmer.

Cook for 15 minutes longer.

Italian Vidalia Onion Soup

Ingredients

2 tablespoons extra virgin olive oil 2 Vidalia onions, minced

1 small carrot, peeled and thinly sliced 1 celery rib, thinly sliced

1/2 teaspoon Italian seasoning 2 cups vegetable stock

1/4 cup red wine vinegar

Heat the oil over medium-high heat.

Sauté red onions until tender for about 5 minutes. Slowly add carrots, celery, and Italian seasoning

Cook for another 5 minutes, or until carrots become tender. Add vegetable stock and red wine vinegar

Boil and simmer.

Cook for 15 minutes longer.

French Red Soup

Ingredients

2 tablespoons olive oil

2 large red onions, minced

1 small turnip, peeled and thinly sliced 1 celery rib, thinly sliced

1/2 teaspoon herbs de Provence 1 cup vegetable stock

1 cup vegetable broth 1/4 cup wine vinegar

Heat the oil over medium-high heat.

Sauté red onions until tender for about 5 minutes. Slowly add turnip, celery, and herbs de Provence

Cook for another 5 minutes, or until turnip become tender. Add vegetable broth, stock and vinegar

Boil and simmer.

Cook for 15 minutes longer.

French Parsnip and Tarragon Soup

Ingredients

2 tablespoons extra virgin olive oil 1 small red onion, minced

1 large parsnip, peeled and thinly sliced 1/2 teaspoon dried tarragon

2 cups vegetable stock 1/4 cup wine vinegar

Heat the oil over medium-high heat.

Sauté red onions until tender for about 5 minutes. Slowly add parsnip and tarragon

Cook for another 5 minutes, or until carrots become tender. Add vegetable broth and vinegar

Boil and simmer.

Cook for 15 minutes longer.

Vidalia Onion and Parsnip Soup2 tablespoons extra virgin olive oil3 Vidalia onions, minced

Ingredients

1 small parsnip, peeled and thinly sliced 1 celery rib, thinly sliced

1/2 teaspoon dried tarragon 2 cups vegetable stock

1/4 cup wine vinegar

Heat the oil over medium-high heat.

Sauté red onions until tender for about 5 minutes. Slowly add parsnip, celery, and tarragon

Cook for another 5 minutes, or until carrots become tender. Add vegetable broth and vinegar

Boil and simmer.

Cook for 15 minutes longer.

Pesto Carrot and Turnip Soup

Ingredients

2 tablespoons extra virgin olive oil 1 small red onion, minced

1 medium carrot, peeled and thinly sliced 1 small turnip, peeled and thinly sliced 1/2 teaspoon dried Italian herbs

1 cup vegetable stock 1 cup vegetable broth 2 tbsp. pesto

1/4 cup wine vinegar

Heat the oil over medium-high heat.

Sauté red onions until tender for about 5 minutes. Slowly add carrots, turnip, and Italian herbs

Cook for another 5 minutes, or until carrots become tender. Add vegetable broth, stock, pesto and vinegar

Boil and simmer.

Cook for 15 minutes longer.

Salad Tomato and Carrot Soup

Ingredients

2 tablespoons olive oil

1 small red onion, minced

1 small carrot, peeled and thinly sliced 2 large Salad tomatoes, thinly sliced 1/2 teaspoon minced ginger

2 sprigs lemon grass

2 cups vegetable broth 2 tbsp. vinegar

Heat the oil over medium-high heat.

Sauté red onions until tender for about 5 minutes.

Slowly add carrots, minced ginger, tomato, and lemon grass Cook for another 5 minutes, or until carrots become tender. Add vegetable broth and vinegar

Boil and simmer.

Cook for 15 minutes longer.

Red Onion Turnip Soup

Ingredients

2 tablespoons sesame seed oil 1 small red onion, minced

1 large turnip, peeled and thinly sliced 2 tsp. chili garlic paste

1/2 teaspoon minced ginger 2 cups vegetable broth

2 tbsp. dry sherry

2 tbsp. distilled white vinegar 1 tsp. soy sauce

Heat the oil over medium-high heat.

Sauté red onions until tender for about 5 minutes.

Slowly add turnip, minced ginger, soy sauce, and chili garlic paste Cook for another 5 minutes, or until carrots become tender.

Add vegetable broth, dry sherry and vinegar Boil and

simmer.

Cook for 15 minutes longer.

Baby Potato and Garbanzo Bean Soup

Ingredients

2 cups baby potatoes

3 tablespoons extra virgin olive oil, divided 2 ¼ cups cherry tomatoes

2 cups 1-inch cut fresh green beans 6 cloves garlic, minced

2 teaspoons dried basil

1 teaspoon flaked kosher salt

1 (15 ounce) can garbanzo beans drained and rinsed 2 teaspoons extra-virgin olive oil, or to taste (optional) Sea salt

Black pepper to taste

Preheat your oven to 425 degrees F (220 degrees C). Line a baking pan with aluminum foil.

Combine potatoes with 1 tablespoon olive oil in a medium bowl. Pour into the baking pan.

Roast in the oven until tender, for about 30 minutes.

Combine the cherry tomatoes, green beans, garlic, basil, and sea salt with 2 tablespoons of olive oil.

Take potatoes out of the oven Push them to one side of the pan.

Add the cherry tomato and green bean mixture.

Roast until the tomatoes begin to wilt, for about 18 min. Take it out of the oven and pour into a dish.

Add the garbanzo beans, 2 teaspoons olive oil, and season with salt and pepper.

Roasted Sweet Potatoes and Green Bean Soup

Ingredients

2 cups sweet potatoes

3 tablespoons extra virgin olive oil, divided 2 ¼ cups cherry tomatoes

2 cups 1-inch cut fresh green beans 8 cloves garlic, minced

2 teaspoons dried basil 1 teaspoon sea salt

1 (15 ounce) can lima beans, drained and rinsed

2 teaspoons extra-virgin olive oil, or to taste (optional) Sea salt

Rainbow peppercorns to taste, finely ground

Preheat your oven to 425 degrees F (220 degrees C). Line a baking pan with aluminum foil.

Combine sweet potatoes with 1 tablespoon olive oil in a

medium bowl.

Pour into the baking pan.

Roast in the oven until tender, for about 30 minutes.

Combine the cherry tomatoes, green beans, garlic, basil, and sea salt with 2 tablespoons of olive oil.

Take potatoes out of the oven Push them to one side of the pan.

Add the cherry tomato and green bean mixture.

Roast until the tomatoes begin to wilt, for about 18 min. Take it out of the oven and pour into a dish.

Add the kidney beans, 2 teaspoons olive oil, and season with sea salt and rainbow peppercorns.

French Baby Potato and Chick Pea Soup

Ingredients

2 cups baby potatoes

3 tablespoons extra virgin olive oil, divided 2 ¼ cups Roma tomatoes

2 cups 1-inch cut fresh green beans 9 cloves garlic, minced

2 teaspoons herbs de Provence 1 teaspoon sea salt

1 (15 ounce) can chick peas, drained and rinsed

2 teaspoons extra-virgin olive oil, or to taste (optional) Sea salt

Black pepper to taste

Preheat your oven to 425 degrees F (220 degrees C). Line a baking pan with aluminum foil.

Combine potatoes with 1 tablespoon olive oil in a medium

bowl. Pour into the baking pan.

Roast in the oven until tender, for about 30 minutes. Combine the cherry tomatoes, green beans, garlic, herbs de Provence, and sea salt with 2 tablespoons of olive oil.

Take potatoes out of the oven Push them to one side of the pan.

Add the cherry tomato and green bean mixture.

Roast until the tomatoes begin to wilt, for about 18 min. Take it out of the oven and pour into a dish.

Add the garbanzo beans, 2 teaspoons olive oil, and season with salt and pepper.

Spicy Tomato and Sweet Potato Soup

Ingredients

2 cups sweet potatoes

3 tablespoons sesame seed oil, divided 2 ¼ cups grape tomatoes

2 cups 1-inch cut fresh green beans 9 cloves garlic, minced

2 teaspoons cayenne pepper 1 teaspoon sea salt

1 (15 ounce) can black beans, drained and rinsed 2

teaspoons sesame oil, or to taste (optional) Sea salt

Black pepper to taste Sesame seeds for garnish

Preheat your oven to 425 degrees F (220 degrees C). Line a baking pan with aluminum foil.

Combine sweet potatoes with 1 tablespoon sesame seed oil in a medium bowl.

Pour into the baking pan.

Roast in the oven until tender, for about 30 minutes.

Combine the cherry tomatoes, green beans, garlic, cayenne pepper, and sea salt with 2 tablespoons of sesame oil.

Take potatoes out of the oven Push them to one side of the pan.

Add the cherry tomato and green bean mixture.

Roast until the tomatoes begin to wilt, for about 18 min.

Take it out of the oven and pour into a dish.

Add the black beans, 2 teaspoons sesame oil, and season with salt and pepper.

Garnish with sesame seeds

Conclusion

We have now reached the end of this fantastic cookbook, I hope it has been to your liking and has met your expectations.

Our book of soups besides being great for leaking ideas for our dishes also cares about our physical fitness, in fact in order to reap all the benefits of the vegetarian diet I would also recommend some physical activity so as to achieve the right balance between body and spirit.

I send you a big hug and hope to keep you company with our vegetarian recipes

CPSIA information can be obtained
at www.ICGtesting.com
Printed in the USA
LVHW060845140621
689681LV00045B/2097